WILD COLOURS

The subtle hue of a Prairie Crocus contrasts with the blazing blooms of Shooting Stars (frontispiece).

A midsummer meadow flourishes near the foot of the Rockwall, Kootenay National Park -- red and pink Indian Paintbrush, yellow Arnicas, pale pink Valerian, and the fluffy seedheads of Western Anemone (right).

A profusion of Wild Roses erupts along the forest's edge in June (left).

The delicate blooms of Western Canada Violets grace the woods in spring (above).

WILD COLOURS

Canada's Rocky Mountain Wildflowers

Paul Gilbert

Photography by Paul Gilbert

Text by Kathryn Graham

Wild Light Press

Canadian Cataloguing in Publication Data

Gilbert, Paul
Wild colours

ISBN 0-9695737-1-5

1. Wild flowers--Rocky Mountains, Canadian (B.C. and Alta.)--Pictorial works.
2. Rocky Mountains, Canadian (B.C.and Alta.)--Pictorial works.
I. Graham, Kathryn   II. Title

QK203.R63G54 1996   582.13'09711   C95-911242-1

Printed and bound in Canada
Printed on acid-free paper

First Printing 1996
Second Printing 1997

Wild Light Press
135-4800 No. 3 Rd., Suite 125
Richmond, B.C. V6X 3A6

A crazy quilt of summer wildflowers basks in the sunset glow, Jasper National Park --
peach and red Indian Paintbrush, yellow Arnicas, mauve Fleabane, Western Anemone seedheads,
white Mountain Heather (preceding page).

An island of Mountain Marsh Marigolds seems to float in an alpine tarn, Banff National Park (right).

A cheerful mix of Ox-eye Daisies, red Indian Paintbrush and bright pink Fireweed enlivens the roadside.

The flamboyant flowers of Wild Bergamot colour the open prairie in Waterton Lakes National Park.

In the soft light of early morning, a pair of Mule Deer rest in a colourful bed of summer wildflowers.

PREFACE

Is it possible to spend time in the Rocky Mountains without becoming bewitched by wildflowers? Although you may come to see the lofty peaks, the turquoise lakes and the glaciers, could you possibly leave without memories coloured by all manner of blooms -- blazing from the roadsides, dancing on the riverbanks, blanketing alpine meadows, defying the barrenness of rock, glowing from the forest floor?

Beyond the obvious appeal of the flawless design of a tiny bloom, or the riot of colour that emblazons a mountain slope, what is the explanation for this enchantment?

In a world dominated by rock and ice, sun and wind, time and space, wildflowers offer us something on a more human scale. We can watch and comprehend the cycles of their lives, identify with their struggle to survive in a vast and unforgiving landscape. And we can applaud their persistence, marvel at their fragile beauty. In fact, it is their impermanence and vulnerability that offer us a perfect counterpoint for appreciating the timeless expanse of the Rocky Mountain wilderness.

Then there is the thrill of finding ourselves -- through good luck or good management -- in exactly the right place at the right time. The quiet enjoyment of a cultivated plot can never rival the excitement of happening upon a wildflower garden flourishing in some unexpected spot, or of arriving in a mountain meadow to discover a sea of colour dancing in the wind. Recognizing the serendipity of such moments only burns them all the more intensely into our memories.

Over the years that Paul and I have spent hiking and exploring in the Rockies, we have fallen under the wildflowers' spell. We have become hunters of beauty, seekers of colour, followers of light. We move quietly through the forests and meadows, watching, looking, searching. We sniff the wind. We read the sky. We depend on intuition.

For the rewards of a flower hunter are great, and as varied as the blooms themselves -- from discovering one tiny perfect plant thriving in stark surroundings, to coming across a cluster of orchids spilling down a mossy slope, to hiking through an alpine meadow that is alive with colour and movement from ankle to infinity. Such floral highlights can only enhance the other aspects of a Rocky Mountain experience: catching a crescent moon sinking in the western sky just before dawn; casual encounters with a deer or a grizzly bear along the trail; hurrying from a high ridge in the face of an advancing thunderstorm; experiencing the immense silence of early morning in backcountry; the sweet song of a thrush; the rumble of an avalanche in the summer heat; deep breaths of crisp air, scented with evergreen; and the cold, cold water of a mountain stream.

But it is for the flowers that we keep returning, following the waxing and the waning of the seasons, year after year. For instead of the predictable replay of previous delights, we have discovered the subtle differences between blooms, and the individual character of every new season. And so our time spent in the Rocky Mountains has taken on its own unique topography, with peaks and valleys coloured by our personal experiences. This book presents some of those moments for you. Enjoy!

-- Kathryn Graham

The warm rays of the setting sun illuminate the golden blooms of Balsamroot that emblazon the hillsides near Waterton Lakes National Park (right).

Wildflowers create bright splashes of colour beside a mountain stream -- pink River Beauty, yellow and red Indian Paintbrush, Yellow Hedysarum, white Grass-of-Parnassus (following pages).

$\mathcal{I}$n the Rocky Mountains, winter is the dominant season, asserting its powerful influence for more than half the year. As the strengthening sun and lengthening days force it out of the valley bottoms, winter takes its leave reluctantly, moving slowly up the mountainsides to the peaks and shaded cracks and crevices where it lurks throughout the summer.

Meanwhile, the warmth and wetness of spring work their magic down below, and gradual greening transforms the landscape. Prairie Crocus open soft purple blooms on the grasslands. Soon the sunny blaze of Balsamroot dots the open hillsides. Meanwhile Calypso Orchids appear in the mossy understory of the forests, plus pure white Western Canada Violets.

Spring is in full swing by late May or early June. Yellow Lady's Slippers and Small Round-leaved Orchids emerge in shaded woods. Dwarf Canadian Primrose pop up in moist and mossy glades, while Spring Beauties spill across grasslands and spangle open forests. Shooting Stars open their bright blooms along rivers and in low-lying mountain meadows. On a few dry slopes a tall and rare orchid appears -- the elegant White Mountain Lady's Slipper.

Early spring in the Canadian Rockies can be an exhilarating experience for flower hunters, as the kaleidoscope of colourful wildflowers unfolds. It can also be a frustrating time, since the season advances slowly, hiking is limited to lower elevations, and many of the blooms are tiny. But with patience and perserverance the hiding spots of many shy beauties can be discovered, their charming presence providing the high point in a day spent rambling through the fresh and fragrant landscape.

The exotic blooms of the Yellow Lady's Slipper, with their plump lips and long twisted petals, are among the showiest of the Rocky Mountain orchids (right).

The sensuous beauty of the orchid can be found in a variety of shapes and sizes in the Canadian Rockies -- from the uncommon flowers of the tall White Mountain Lady's Slipper (left) to the cheerful cluster of tiny blooms that make up a Small Round-leaved Orchid (above).

Raindrops decorate the unfolding flower of a Glacier Lily
(above).

Often found in clumps of six or more, a lively group of
Calypso Orchids dances before the fresh bloom of a
Glacier Lily (right).

One of the most elegant Rocky Mountain wildflowers is the Western Wood Lily, although its classic blooms become rarer each year due to thoughtless picking.

Water droplets on Dwarf Canadian Primrose capture and reflect the diminutive blooms and their mountain environment.

A Columbian Ground Squirrel pauses momentarily in a golden patch of Glacier Lilies (above).

The brilliant yellow blooms of Glacier Lilies carpet the forest floor in spring (right).

*B*y late June, spring is well entrenched at lower elevations in the Rockies, and it has worked its way up the mountainsides to establish a foothold above the treeline. Climbing up to the alpine, hikers pass through woodlands dotted with a multitude of tiny yellow Evergreen Violets and slog through the last stubborn snowdrifts. Their reward is the cheerful display of wildflowers that carpets the high forests and meadows.

Glacier Lilies, along with Western Anemones and Globe Flowers, are often found growing near shrinking snowbanks, and sometimes in their impatience, push up through the snow before it has had time to melt. The brilliant Glacier Lilies have delicate blooms, with shy curling petals and heads that nod demurely. But en masse, their effect is powerful, breathtaking. Hiking up above the treeline on a sunny spring day and finding the slopes awash with warm yellow blooms makes winter seem very far away indeed.

In the valley forests and meadows, the early spring wildflowers have given way to the late spring blooms. Western Wood Lilies erupt along roadsides and in open glades, while Blue Camas blanket wet depressions on the prairies. Mariposa Lilies hide among the grasses, but blue Lupines and Sticky Purple Geraniums create colourful splashes across the landscape.

As June slides into July, the symmetrical blooms of Bunchberry Dogwoods and tiny Twinflowers start to appear in the forests, a sure sign that summer is just around the corner.

Spring's arrival in the high country is celebrated by slopes ablaze with the sunny blooms of Glacier Lilies, Yoho National Park (right).

Two of the most common and symmetrical wildflowers found in Rocky Mountain forests -- petite pink Twinflowers (above) and pure white Bunchberry Dogwoods (right).

Blue Camas (left) and Evergreen Violets (above) sport similar colours in very different designs.

Soft light illuminates a scene reminiscent of a watercolour painting -- a miniature forest of blue Lupines among the creamy trunks of Aspens.

The fresh flowers of the Spring Beauty often have brightly coloured anthers and veins (left).

One of the most unusual wildflowers of the Canadian Rockies is the Shooting Star -- each bloom is like an individual spark: yellow-hot in the centre with a tail of flaming pink or purple (right).

Marmots play in a meadow where a Western Anemone blooms, soon after the snow has receded (left).

Spring sun highlights a solitary Western Anemone and a cheery patch of Glacier Lilies (right).

The splendour of a sunny summer's day in Waterton Lakes National Park -- Sticky Purple Geraniums, blue Lupines, yellow Prairie Groundsel, white Northern Bedstraw, Mariposa Lilies, Harebells, Yarrow.

A raindrop on the bright bud of a Wild Rose mirrors the innocent face of a nearby bloom (left).

On a cool and fresh morning in July, dewdrops sparkle on the delicate flowers of Blue Clematis (above).

Able to thrive in some of the most unlikely places, a clump of Spotted Saxifrage clings to a rocky mountainside (far left).

A close look reveals the whimsical blooms that inspired the name Elephanthead (left).

*A*s spring makes its soft transition into summer, the possibilities for flower hunters expand and become more diverse. Beautiful blooms can be found everywhere in the Rocky Mountain landscape -- from the roadsides to the forests, the rocky slopes and the high country.

The last few Brown-eyed Susans mingle with the burgeoning Wild Bergamot and Harebells. In moist meadows and along alpine lakeshores, Mountain Marsh Marigold and Elephanthead emerge, while Blue Clematis trail across open slopes.

Along the roads there is an ever-changing crazy quilt of blooms -- Wild Roses, Indian Paintbrush, Fireweed, Locoweed. Bright bunches of River Beauty add a dash of colour to streams and gravel flats.

Hikers can delight in the graceful Yellow Columbines nodding along the trails, or search out the tall feathery plumes of Beargrass that dot the mountainsides in the southern Rockies.

By late July or early August, the wildflowers in the high meadows are at their peak, creating one of the most striking spectacles to be found anywhere. A profusion of lively blooms opens to carpet the landscape with dancing colour -- a vibrant mosaic as far as the eye can see. The sunny yellow of the Arnicas and the light purple of the Fleabanes are interspersed with the myriad hues of the Indian Paintbrush -- everything from gaudy reds and oranges to elegant pinks, cool yellow-green and almost translucent white. Here and there are sprinkled the cheery blue Alpine Forget-Me-Nots and the miniature bells of Mountain Heather, while the fuzzy seedheads of the Western Anemones add a comic touch. Each meadow has its own unique combination of colours and blooms, dazzling displays that many wildflower enthusiasts consider to be the floral high point of the year.

The graceful flowers of a Yellow Columbine float in front of a peaceful background, created by the warm glow of a summer's evening reflected in Emerald Lake, Yoho National Park (right).

Early morning in backcountry -- Fireweed and Ragwort crowd along the shore of Rock Isle Lake, Mount Assiniboine Provincial Park.

Creamy plumes of Beargrass stretch skyward on a beautiful summer's day in Waterton Lakes National Park, dwarfing nearby purple Asters and red Indian Paintbrush.

*The full presence of summer is marked by the vivid blooming of Fireweed,
with the rugged Sawback Range of Banff National Park as a backdrop.*

The bold red of Indian Paintbrush contrasts sharply with the icy blue of the rushing Vermilion River, Kootenay National Park (above).

Lush meadows spring up in midsummer in view of the Angel Glacier on Mount Edith Cavell, Jasper National Park -- peach and red Indian Paintbrush, yellow Arnicas, mauve Fleabane, white Mountain Heather (right).

Thick wildflowers blanket the slopes with lively colour --
mauve Fleabane, yellow Arnicas, red and variegated Indian Paintbrush,
Wood Betony, the seedpods of Glacier Lilies (left).

A sprinkling of Arnicas surrounds the weathered form of a fallen tree
(below).

An intimate portrait of a friendly pair of Harebells (above).

Bright bunches of River Beauty line the banks of a mountain stream (right).

The bold blooms of Shrubby Cinquefoil form a sunny border along the shore of Lake Louise, Banff National Park (left).

By August, the intense colours of Monkeyflowers can be found glowing in moist glades, often near ice-cold mountain streams (above).

$\mathcal{T}$he passage of summer is marked by decreasing daylight and the spirited blooming of alpine wildflowers. By the last full days of the season, it has climbed the mountainsides to decorate the highest ridges and peaks. Beautiful hanging gardens appear at dizzying heights, wherever they can get a toehold in the barren and rocky landscape. It is always surprising to hike up and up and up to the unforgiving alpine and be greeted by tiny blooms flashing intense pinks, bright yellows, innocent whites and delicate blues.

The small size of these blossoms belies their strength and tenacity in the face of the blistering sun, the persistent winds, and the very possible visit of winter on any day of the year. Each plant has developed its own special strategies for survival in an environment where the temperature ranges can be extreme and the growing season quite short. Moss Campion is able to thrive under such difficult conditions, due to a long taproot and tight cushion growth, so these mossy mats studded with sprightly pink blooms flourish throughout the Rockies. Equally hardy are the Saxifrages, which also take advantage of cushion growth to push their seemingly fragile flowers skyward on rocky slopes and ledges. Creeping Beardtongue hugs the rugged soil and produces masses of handsome blooms among its leathery leaves, while the jaunty Alpine Forget-Me-Nots wear a thick coat of hairs to protect them from the elements.

As August fades into September, summer increasingly loses ground in its tug-of-war with winter. Fresh snow dusts the peaks and night-time temperatures plummet, leaving only the toughest and most sheltered plants unscathed. The blazing yellows and reds of autumn bring final proof of summer's demise. The wonderful wildflowers that graced the Rocky Mountain landscape are gone, persisting only in the dormant seeds, bulbs and roots that will burst into life another year. But in our minds they live on too, filling our memories, our imaginations, and our dreams with colours and scents, whetting our appetites for another season of flower hunting.

A summer snowstorm approaches the high ridge where a hardy bunch of Spotted Saxifrage has made a home, overlooking the Lineham Lakes, Waterton Lakes National Park (right).

*In the lee of the winds at Carthew Pass, a gallant group of plants
beautifies the harsh alpine environment -- Spotted Saxifrage,
yellow Cinquefoil, and purple Creeping Beardtongue,
Waterton Lakes National Park (left).*

*Yellow Mountain Saxifrage sprouts bright blooms in the middle of
a stony still life (above).*

Bright cushions of Moss Campion, studded with starry pink blooms, often entrench themselves in rocky alpine locales (left).

Looking up from below, it is hard to believe that any wildflowers can survive on the rugged slopes of mountains such as Mount Huber, Yoho National Park (right).

Lovely variations of the ubiquitous Indian Paintbrush (above).

A multitude of vivid wildflowers crowds a high mountain meadow -- red, pink, yellow, white and variegated Indian Paintbrush, blue Alpine Forget-Me-Nots, yellow Arnicas, pale pink Valerian, and the fluffy seedheads of Western Anemone (right),

HINTS FOR FLOWER HUNTERS

Since many wildflower enthusiasts enjoy naming, classifying and learning about flora in addition to appreciating their visual beauty, a mini-guide to the flowers pictured in this book has been compiled. It provides information about when and where to look for specific flowers, plus interesting notes about certain plants. It does not attempt, however, to cover the full scope of Rocky Mountain wildflowers. Serious flower hunters will want to purchase one of the excellent guidebooks that are available.

Vertical variations in the landscape and the northwest-southeast march of the Rocky Mountain range make the search for wildflowers a varied and challenging experience. To be successful, it is important to become aware of the influences that altitude, latitude, precipitation and exposure have on flora. These elements, along with other variables such as soil and prevailing winds, determine the plant growth in any given location in the Rockies.

In general, flowers begin to grow earlier and become taller at lower elevations, while late season blooms are often able to survive longer into the fall. As one ascends the mountainsides, the same flowers are found sprouting later and maturing at a smaller size, with a shorter growing season. Thus a flower such as the Indian Paintbrush can be found blooming in the valleys from June through September and may grow as tall as 60 cm there, while in alpine meadows it may only bloom during August and reach a maximum height of 10 cm.

In the Canadian Rockies, there are three vegetation zones that are defined by altitude: montane, subalpine and alpine. Above the alpine zone there is only bare rock or permanent snow and ice. Different flowers may be found growing in one, two or all three zones.

Montane -- This is the lowest zone in terms of elevation, generally found in the valley bottoms. It is the warmest and driest zone, with the longest growing season.

Subalpine -- This is the middle zone, consisting mainly of treed slopes. It is cooler, wetter and windier than the montane, with a shorter growing season.

Alpine -- This is the highest zone, located above the treeline. It has the coolest, wettest and windiest conditions, plus the shortest growing season. Plants found here need special adaptations to help them survive.

Monkeyflowers

The photographs for this book were taken in the southern portion of the Canadian Rocky Mountains, in an area that includes a number of national parks: Waterton Lakes, Banff, Kootenay, Yoho and Jasper. This region spans about four degrees of latitude, so there are considerable variations in flora. In the southern part of the range included, a greater variety of wildflowers can be found, and all of the vegetation zones extend to higher elevations. The treeline is found at an elevation of about 2300 m in the south and at about 2000 m in the north. A number of arctic plants can be found in the northern part of the area.

Precipitation varies with altitude, the lower areas being drier and the higher areas wetter. This, in part, accounts for the lush summer growth in alpine meadows. As well, the western side of the Rockies receives more precipitation, which allows more trees to grow and supports a greater variety of plants. Meanwhile, the eastern side is often in a rain shadow, which results in fewer trees, more sparse vegetation and more extreme temperature ranges.

The differing exposure to sunlight between north and south-facing slopes also has an impact on vegetation. South-facing slopes receive more sunlight and become clear of snow earlier. These warmer conditions allow more growth and a higher treeline than on the cooler, more shaded north-facing slopes.

With a rudimentary understanding of the influences that altitude, latitude, precipitation and exposure have on the flora of the Canadian Rockies, wildflower enthusiasts should be ready to take to the trail and try their luck. Happy hunting!

Alpine Forget-Me-Not   Borage Family
Latin names: Myosotis alpestris, M. sylvatica
Other common names:
Habitat: Subalpine and Alpine zones --
    moist meadows, bare slopes,
    mostly above treeline
Flowering Season: July - August
Height: 5 - 20 cm
Of interest: Its flowers are quite fragrant.
    It is the official state flower of Alaska.

Arnica   Composite Family
Latin names: Arnica cordifolia, A. mollis
Other common names: Heartleaf Arnica
Habitat: Subalpine and Alpine zones --
    open forest, moist areas,
    near or above treeline
Flowering Season: June - August
Height: 15 - 70 cm
Of interest: There are about 15 species of
    Arnica in the Canadian Rockies.

Aster
Composite Family

Latin names: Aster subspicatus, A.foliaceus, A. laevis
Other common names: Leafy Aster, Smooth Aster, Mountain Aster
Habitat: Subalpine and Alpine zones -- open woods, dry slopes
Flowering Season: July - September
Height: 30 - 100 cm
Of interest: Many insects are attracted to Asters, especially bumblebees and butterflies.
    Asters are very difficult to identify, not only to differentiate between different kinds of Asters, but also to tell from Fleabanes.

Balsamroot
Composite Family

Latin name: Balsamorhiza sagittata
Other common names:
Habitat: Montane and Subalpine zones -- open sunny areas, grassy hills
Flowering Season: May - June
Height: 30 - 60 cm
Of interest: It is found only in the most southern parts of the Canadian Rockies.
    It was an important food source for native people, and it is eaten by deer, elk and mountain sheep.

Beargrass
Lily Family

Latin name: Xerophyllum tenax
Other common names: Elk-grass, Basket-grass
Habitat: Subalpine and Alpine zones -- dry slopes and meadows
Flowering Season: June - August
Height: 50 - 150 cm
Of interest: Bears eat the leaf bases in the spring; mountain goats eat the leaves in winter; and elk, deer and mountain sheep eat the stems and flowers.
    Natives wove baskets and clothing from the leaves.

Blue Camas
Lily Family

Latin name: Camassia quamash
Other common names: Wild Hyacinth, Purple Camas, Early Camas
Habitat: Montane zone -- wet meadows, stream banks
Flowering Season: May - July
Height: 30 -60 cm
Of interest: It grows only in the most southern part of the Canadian Rockies.
    The bulbs were a very important food source for natives. They were prepared and eaten in many ways.

Blue Clematis
Buttercup Family

Latin name: Clematis columbiana
Other common names: Purple Virgin's Bower
Habitat: Subalpine zone -- open woods and thickets
Flowering Season: May - July
Height: 10 - 20 cm
Of interest: It is one of the few trailing or climbing vines to be found in the Canadian Rockies.

Brown-eyed Susan
Composite Family

Latin name: Gaillardia aristata
Other common names: Wild Gaillardia
Habitat: Montane zone -- dry grasslands, open sunny areas

Brown-eyed Susans

Flowering Season: June - August
Height: 30 - 80 cm
Of interest: There is some disagreement as to whether it is a true Brown-eyed Susan.

Bunchberry Dogwood
Dogwood Family

Latin name: Cornus canadensis
Other common names: Dwarf Dogwood
Habitat: Montane and Subalpine zones -- moist coniferous forests
Flowering Season: June - July
Height: 5 - 20 cm
Of interest: It grows throughout much of Canada, North America and eastern Asia.
    The leaves turn red and purple in fall.
    The leaves are eaten by deer, and the berries are eaten by grouse and other birds.

Calypso Orchid
Orchid Family

Latin name: Calypso bulbosa
Other common names: Fairy Slipper, Venus Slipper, Deer Orchid
Habitat: Montane and Subalpine zones -- shaded forest, mossy areas
Flowering Season: May - July
Height: 8 - 12 cm
Of interest: Their root systems are quite fragile, and the entire plant is often destroyed if the flower is picked.

Cinquefoil
Rose Family

Latin name: Potentilla diversifolia
Other common names: Mountain Meadow Cinquefoil
Habitat: Subalpine and Alpine zones -- high rocky ledges, alpine herbmats
Flowering Season: June - August
Height: 10 - 50 cm
Of interest: It is a common and highly variable plant.

Cow Parsnip
Carrot or Parsnip Family

Latin name: Heracleum lanatum
Other common names: Common Cow Parsnip
Habitat: Montane and Subalpine zones -- damp meadows, moist forests, avalanche slopes
Flowering Season: July - August
Height: 100 - 250 cm
Of interest: The flowers and fruits have a unique odour, strong but not unpleasant.
    The seeds, flowers and leaves are eaten by a number of different animals.

Creeping Beardtongue
Figwort Family

Latin name: Penstemon ellipticus
Other common names: Shrubby Beardtongue, Shrubby Penstemon
Habitat: Subalpine and Alpine zones -- dry rocky slopes, scree
Flowering Season: July - August
Height: 10 - 45 cm
Of interest: It is semi-evergreen -- some of its leaves turn red and drop in the fall.
    Of at least a dozen species of Penstemon in the Canadian Rockies, a few are unique to the region.

Dwarf Canadian Primrose
Primrose Family

Latin name: Primula mistassinica
Other common names: Bird's-eye Primrose
Habitat: Montane zone -- wet calcareous soil by water
Flowering Season: June
Height: 10 - 15 cm
Of interest: It often grows in small colonies around a mother plant.

Elephanthead
Figwort Family

Latin name: Pedicularis groenlandica
Other common names: Elephant's Head
Habitat: Montane, Subalpine and Alpine --
wet meadows, marshes, stream banks
Flowering Season: June - August
Height: 30 - 60 cm
Of interest: Both the leaves and stems can
be a purple colour.

Evergreen Violet
Violet Family

Latin name: Viola orbiculata
Other common names: Yellow Violet,
Round-leaved Violet
Habitat: Montane, Subalpine and Alpine --
moist woods, mossy areas
Flowering Season: May - July
Height: 3 - 6 cm
Of interest: Its leaves remain green through-
out the winter.

Fireweed
Evening Primrose Family

Latin name: Epilobium angustifolium
Other common names: Great Willow-herb
Habitat: Montane, Subalpine and Alpine --
dry open areas, burnt or disturbed sites
Flowering Season: July - August
Height: 20 - 200 cm
Of interest: It is a favourite food of grizzly
bears, and is also eaten by deer and elk.

Fleabane
Composite Family

Latin name: Erigeron peregrinus
Other common names: Tall Purple Fleabane,
Showy Fleabane, Mountain Erigeron
Habitat: Subalpine and Alpine zones --
open woods and meadows
Flowering Season: July - August
Height: 25 - 70 cm
Of interest: Fleabanes are quite similar to
Asters, and equally difficult to identify
correctly.

Glacier Lily
Lily Family

Latin name: Erythronium grandiflorum
Other common names: Yellow Avalanche Lily,
Snow Lily
Habitat: Montane, Subalpine and Alpine --
open forests, alpine meadows
Flowering Season: May - July
Height: 15 - 30 cm
Of interest: The bulbs are dug up and eaten
by black and grizzly bears and small
rodents. The seed pods are eaten by
deer, elk, sheep and goats.
The natives used the bulbs as a winter
food.

Globe Flowers
Buttercup Family

Latin names: Trollius albiflorus, T. laxus
Other common names: White Globe Flower
Habitat: Subalpine and Alpine zones --
wet meadows, marshy areas,
stream banks, near melting snow
Flowering Season: May - August
Height: 15 - 30 cm

Golden Fleabane
Composite Family

Latin name: Erigeron aureus
Habitat: Alpine zone --
turfy alpine slopes
Flowering Season: July - August
Height: 2 - 15 cm
Of interest: It is a dwarf species, with the
flower head appearing large compared to
the rest of the plant.

Grass-of-Parnassus
Saxifrage Family

Latin name: Parnassia fimbriata
Other common names: Fringed Grass-of-Parnassus
Habitat: Montane, Subalpine and Alpine --
wet mossy areas, coniferous forests
Flowering Season: July - August
Height: 15 - 60 cm
Of interest: It often grows in dense colonies.

Moss Campion and Golden Fleabane

Hairy Golden Aster
Composite Family

Latin names: Chrysopsis [Heterotheca] villosa
Other common names: Golden Aster
Habitat: Montane and Subalpine zones --
dry sunny areas
Flowering Season: July - August
Height: 20 - 30 cm
Of interest: It can endure drought.

Harebell
Harebell or Bluebell Family

Latin name: Campanula rotundifolia
Other common names: Bluebell
Habitat: Montane, Subalpine and Alpine --
open areas, sandy or gravelly soil
Flowering Season: July - August
Height: 10 - 45 cm
Of interest: Occasionally it has white flowers.

Indian Paintbrush
Figwort Family

Latin names: Castilleja miniata, C. rhexifolia,
C. occidentalis
Other common names: Painted Cup
Habitat: Montane, Subalpine and Alpine --
open woods, meadows, roadsides
Flowering Season: June - September
Height: 10 - 60 cm
Of interest: It is very difficult to classify,
since there are more than 10 species in
the Rockies, and many variations of each.
It is semi-parasitic, feeding off the
roots of other plants.
The colourful bracts are not flowers.
Hummingbirds are attracted to the
small tubes, which are the true flowers.

Locoweed
Pea Family

Latin names: Oxytropis campestris,
O. monticola, O. spicata
Other common names: Late Yellow Locoweed
Habitat: Montane and Subalpine zones --
dry open areas
Flowering Season: July - August
Height: 10 - 30 cm
Of interest: Another highly variable plant, it
can be yellowish-white, white, blue, pink
or purple.

Lupine
Pea Family

Latin names: Lupinus sericeus, L. minimus
Other common names: Silky Lupine,
Dwarf Lupine
Habitat: Montane zone --
meadows, dry prairie, grasslands,
forest openings
Flowering Season: June - August
Height: 20 - 50 cm
Of interest: Lupines are only found in the
most southern part of the Canadian
Rockies.

Mariposa Lily
Lily Family

Latin name: Calochortus apiculatus
Other common names: Pointed Mariposa Lily
Habitat: Montane zone --
grasslands, prairie, open sunny forest
Flowering Season: May - July
Height: 10 - 20 cm
Of interest: It is only found in the southern-
most part of the Canadian Rockies.
The bulbs were eaten by natives and
early settlers.

Monkeyflower
Figwort Family

Latin name: Mimulus lewissi
Other common names: Red Monkeyflower
Habitat: Subalpine zone --
open wet areas, near cold streams
Flowering Season: July - August
Height: 30 - 60 cm
Of interest: Monkeyflowers are only found in
Waterton Lakes and Jasper National Parks.
They often attract hummingbirds and bees.

*A sparkling summer morning at Bow Lake, Banff National Park --
bright pink Fireweed, white Locoweed, yellow Rocky Mountain Goldenrod,
yellow Shrubby Cinquefoil.*

The lacy filigree of Cow Parsnip and the pale shafts of Beargrass
stand out against the blue summer sky, while red Indian Paintbrush
blooms at their feet.

Moss Campion
Pink Family

Latin name: Silene acaulis
Other common names: Carpet Pink, Moss Pink
Habitat: Alpine zone --
rock and thin soil, alpine slopes
Flowering Season: June - August
Height: 2 - 5 cm
Of interest: Moss Campion may be 10 years old before it begins to flower.
It is cross-fertilized by night-flying insects, which are attracted by its scent.

Mountain Heather
Heath Family

Latin names: Cassiope mertensiana, C. tetragona
Other common names: White Mountain Heather
Habitat: Subalpine and Alpine zones --
alpine meadows, near treeline
Flowering Season: July - August
Height: 5 - 15 cm
Of interest: It is actually a dwarf evergreen shrub.
The white variety can hybridize with red and yellow varieties.

Mountain Marsh Marigold
Buttercup Family

Latin name: Caltha leptosepala
Other common names: White Marsh Marigold
Habitat: Subalpine and Alpine zones --
wet meadows, marshes,
near streams and lakes
Flowering Season: July - August
Height: 10 - 20 cm

Northern Bedstraw
Madder Family

Latin name: Galium boreale
Other common names:
Habitat: Montane and Subalpine zones --
dry open areas, forests, roadsides
Flowering Season: June - July
Height: 20 - 50 cm
Of interest: The flowers are quite fragrant.

Ox-eye Daisy
Composite Family

Latin name: Chrysanthemum leucanthemum
Other common names: Daisy
Habitat: Montane zone --
roadsides, disturbed sites
Flowering Season: July - August
Height: 10 - 60 cm
Of interest: Daisies are not native plants.
They are originally from Europe and Asia.

Prairie Crocus
Buttercup Family

Latin names: Anemone patens, A. nuttaliana,
Pulsatilla ludoviciana
Other common names: Pasque Flower, Wild Crocus
Habitat: Montane zone --
grasslands, meadows, open woods
Flowering Season: April - June
Height: 10 - 15 cm
Of interest: It often begins to grow before the snow has melted.
The flowers emerge before the leaves.
It is the floral emblem of Manitoba, and the state flower of South Dakota.

Prairie Groundsel
Composite Family

Latin name: Senecio canus
Other common names: Ragwort
Habitat: Montane and Subalpine zones --
dry open areas, prairies, roadsides
Flowering Season: June - July
Height: 15 - 45 cm
Of interest: Senecio is the largest genus of flowering plants, including more than a thousand species, thirteen of which are found in the Rocky Mountains.

Ragwort
Composite Family

Latin name: Senecio triangularis
Other common names: Giant Ragwort,
Triangular-leaved Ragwort

Globe Flowers

Habitat: Subalpine and Alpine zones --
moist meadows, near water
Flowering Season: July - August
Height: 60 - 150 cm
Of interest: It often grows in large colonies.

River Beauty
Evening Primrose Family

Latin name: Epilobium latifolium
Other common names: Broad-leaved Willow-herb,
Mountain Fireweed, Alpine Fireweed
Habitat: Montane, Subalpine and Alpine --
floodplains, gravel and sandbars
Flowering Season: July - September
Height: 15 - 40 cm
Of interest: The leaves, flowers and buds of River Beauty can be eaten raw or cooked.

Rocky Mountain Goldenrod
Composite Family

Latin name: Solidago multiradiata
Other common names:
Habitat: Montane and Subalpine zones --
dry open areas, near water
Flowering Season: July - August
Height: 5 - 40 cm

Shooting Star
Primrose Family

Latin name: Dodecatheon pulchellum,
D. radicatum, D. pauciflorum
Other common names: Peacock
Habitat: Montane, Subalpine and Alpine --
moist meadows, bogs, near water
Flowering Season: June - July
Height: 10 - 20 cm
Of interest: They are eaten by deer and elk in the early spring when other vegetation is scarce.
If picked, the entire plant is destroyed.

Shrubby Cinquefoil
Rose Family

Latin name: Potentilla fruticosa
Other common names:
Habitat: Montane, Subalpine and Alpine --
dry areas, meadows, alpine slopes
Flowering Season: June - September
Height: 30 - 150 cm
Of interest: It has one of the longest blooming periods of any plant in the Rockies.
Wild animals browse on this flowering shrub , especially in winter.

Small Round-leaved Orchid
Orchid Family

Latin name: Orchis rotundifolia
Other common names: One-leaf Orchid
Habitat: Montane and Subalpine zones --
shaded forest, moist or boggy areas
Flowering Season: June - July
Height: 10 - 25 cm
Of interest: It is an uncommon plant.
The root system is quite fragile, so the plant is usually destroyed if picked.

Spotted Saxifrage
Saxifrage Family

Latin name: Saxifraga bronchialis
Other common names: Prickly Saxifrage
Habitat: Subalpine and Alpine zones --
rock crevices, scree, rocky slopes
Flowering Season: June - August
Height: 5 - 30 cm
Of interest: The name "saxifrage" is derived from the Latin words for "break" and "rock".

Spring Beauty
Purslane Family

Latin name: Claytonia lanceolata
Other common names: Western Spring Beauty
Habitat: Montane, Subalpine and Alpine --
moist areas, meadows, open forests
Flowering Season: April - July
Height: 5 - 15 cm
Of interest: It is one of the earliest bloomers.
Its bulb-like roots are dug up and eaten by grizzly bears and other animals.

Sticky Purple Geranium
Geranium Family
Latin name: Geranium viscosissimum
Other common names: Sticky Purple Cranesbill
Habitat: Montane and Subalpine zones --
    meadows, lightly shaded woods
Flowering Season: June - August
Height: 30 - 60 cm
Of interest: The stems, leaves and parts of
    the flowers are covered with sticky hairs.
    When the seed pods ripen they split
    open, catapulting the seeds away.

Twinflower
Honeysuckle Family
Latin name: Linnaea borealis
Other common names:
Habitat: Subalpine and Alpine zones --
    coniferous forests, cool mossy areas
Flowering Season: July
Height: 5 - 15 cm
Of interest: The leaves of Twinflower are
    evergreen, and the flowers are sweet-
    scented.
    It is found all around the northern
    hemisphere -- Canada, Alaska, Greenland,
    Sweden, Lapland, Russia, China, Japan.

Valerian
Valerian Family
Latin name: Valeriana sitchensis
Other common names: Sitka Valerian,
    Mountain Valerian, Wild Heliotrope
Habitat: Subalpine and Alpine zones --
    moist forests, meadows
Flowering Season: July - August
Height: 40 - 80 cm
Of interest: Although the scent of the flowers
    is unpleasant to humans, the blooms are
    very attractive to insects. The odour
    grows stronger after a frost.

Western Anemone
Buttercup Family
Latin name: Anemone occidentalis
Other common names: White Pasque Flower,
    Wind Flower, Chalice Flower, Towhead Babies
Habitat: Subalpine and Alpine zones --
    wet meadows, near melting snowbanks
Flowering Season: June - July
Height: 10 - 30 cm
Of interest: The flowers develop first, then
    the leaves. They actually begin to grow
    beneath the snow and push up through it.
    The flowers are short-lived, but the
    fluffy seedheads are seen throughout the
    summer.

Western Canada Violet
Violet Family
Latin names: Viola canadensis, V. rugulosa
Other common names: Canada Violet,
    Tall White Violet
Habitat: Montane zone --
    moist open forests
Flowering season: May - July
Height: 7 - 25 cm
Of interest: The ripened seed pods twist open
    suddenly, flinging the seeds away.

Western Wood Lily
Lily Family
Latin names: Lilium philadelphicum,
    L. montanum
Other common names: Wood Lily
Habitat: Montane zone --
    moist meadows, open woods
Flowering Season: June - July
Height: 30 - 60 cm
Of interest: It is the floral emblem of
    Saskatchewan.
    Each plant usually has one or two blooms,
but once in a while they have five or more.
    People who have picked this lovely
flower have wiped it out in certain areas.
Even if the bulb is left in the ground, the
plant can die.

White Mountain Lady's Slipper

White Mountain Lady's Slipper
Orchid Family
Latin name: Cypripedium montanum
Other common names: Moccasin Flower
Habitat: Montane and Subalpine zones --
    open woods, dry slopes
Flowering Season: June - July
Height: 20 - 50 cm
Of interest: It is one of the rarer orchids to be
    found in the Canadian Rockies.

Wild Bergamot
Mint Family
Latin name: Monarda fistulosa
Other common names: Horsemint, Bee Balm
    Wild Bergamont
Habitat: Montane zone --
    prairies, sunny slopes, open woods
Flowering Season: July - August
Height: 20 - 70 cm
Of interest: It grows only in the southern Canadian Rockies.

Wild Rose
Rose Family
Latin names: Rosa acicularis, R. woodsii
Other common names: Prickly Rose
Habitat: Montane and Subalpine zones --
    dry areas, open woods
Flowering Season: June - July
Height: 50 - 150 cm
Of interest: It is the provincial flower of Alberta.

Wood Betony
Figwort Family
Latin name: Pedicularis bracteosa
Other common names: Bracted Lousewort
Habitat: Subalpine and Alpine zones --
    moist meadows, open woods
Flowering Season: June - August
Height: 40 - 100 cm
Of interest: It is semi-parasitic.

Yarrow
Composite Family
Latin names: Achillea millefolium, A. nigrescens
Other common names: Milfoil
Habitat: Montane, Subalpine and Alpine --
    grasslands to alpine areas
Flowering Season: June - August
Height: 20 - 70 cm
Of interest: The leaves of Yarrow are some-
    times mistaken for ferns.

Yellow Columbine
Buttercup Family
Latin name: Aquilegia flavescens
Other common names:
Habitat: Montane, Subalpine and Alpine --
    meadows, open woods, rocky areas, scree
Flowering Season: June - August
Height: 20 - 60 cm
Of interest: Bees, butterflies, insects and
    hummingbirds are attracted to its nectar.

Yellow Hedysarum
Pea Family
Latin name: Hedysarum sulphurescens
Other common names: Yellow Sweetvetch
Habitat: Subalpine and Alpine zones --
    moist open forest, along streams
Flowering Season: June - July
Height: 30 - 60 cm
Of interest: The roots are a very important
    food for grizzly bears in spring and fall.

Yellow Lady's Slipper
Orchid Family
Latin name: Cypripedium calceolus
Other common names: Yellow Moccasin Flower
Habitat: Montane and Subalpine zones --
    moist forest, bogs, gravelly areas
Flowering Season: June - July
Height: 15 - 30 cm

Yellow Mountain Saxifrage
Saxifrage Family
Latin name: Saxifraga aizoides
Other common names:
Habitat: Subalpine and Alpine zones --
    moist sand and gravel, stony areas
Flowering Season: July - August
Height: 5 - 10 cm
Of interest: A close look at the tiny flowers
    reveals that they are spotted with orange.

Nestled among the grasses, a Mariposa Lily displays an elegant beauty.

PHOTOGRAPHER'S NOTE

Summer in the Rockies has always been something I've looked forward to with great anticipation. The enhanced feeling of timelessness, space and solace has, over time, led to a heightened awareness and connection to the landscape. It is my experience that through this saturation of awareness expressive images result.

The inherent risk to all nature photographers is in not putting oneself in the right place at the decisive moment to create an expressive photograph. Research, technical competence and anticipation are all important in wildflower photography; however I feel one must be persistent to achieve creative success.

The shooting of *Wild Colours* was a very physical process. Knowing when and where the flowers are is one thing -- rising at 4:30 in the morning to hike ten kilometres in expectation of perfect light is another.

To ramble over a mountain pass and come upon an alpine meadow in full summer bloom is a spectacular sight. To have the opportunity spoiled by a constant breeze or poor light is a photographer's hell.

Still the challenge beckons. The search for perfect light and flowers continues. Winter dreams of *Wild Colours* will draw me back to the Rockies for years to come.

-- Paul Gilbert

A scene in Banff National Park that incorporates some of the most famous elements of the Canadian Rockies -- the rugged peaks of the Continental Divide, the Crowfoot Glacier, the turquoise waters of Bow Lake, the evergreen forest, and the flashy reds of Indian Paintbrush (left).

TECHNICAL INFORMATION

The pursuit of photographs for this book was as much a pursuit of exceptional light as it was of the wildflowers themselves. As well as understanding the quality of light, wildflower photographers need to do their botanical research, be technically competent, and exercise the art of good composition. In general, early mornings, evenings and overcast days provide the best conditions for wildflower photography.

In order to portray the flowers in a natural context, the use of electronic flash was avoided and only natural light was used. On occasion reflectors were utilized to modulate existing light conditions by adding light to shadowed areas. Neutral density and polarizing filters were also used to reduce glare and control contrast.

To capture the vibrant colours and ensure maximum sharpness and detail, Fuji Velvia 50 film was used in the majority of situations.

A 35mm Canon camera system with lenses ranging from 20mm to 300mm was employed, with the 24mm and the 90mm macro getting the most use. At times, a Pentax 6x7 medium format system was also used.

Maximizing depth of field is often of utmost importance when photographing flowers. Small aperture settings lead to slow shutter speeds, which make a tripod necessary. A sturdy Manfrotto 055 was used to make the majority of photos for this book.

Because wind is a wildflower photographer's greatest nemesis, many otherwise great shots were spoiled due to motion. On less than calm days, as many as a dozen exposures were made of each composition to ensure that a couple of razor sharp images resulted.

And finally, in this age of computer scanning and manipulation, it seems necessary to note that none of the images in *Wild Colours* was digitally altered in any way.

The last light of day illuminates a rich array of wildflowers in
Waterton Lakes National Park -- deep pink Wild Bergamot,
Hairy Golden Asters, blue Harebells, Brown-eyed Susans (right).

Special thanks to our families and friends for their encouragement and support.

Brown-eyed Susans bask in the golden glow of twilight.

Designed by Paul Gilbert and Kathryn Graham
Text edited by Joanne Mitchell, Blue Systems

To inquire about photographic workshops, hiking tours
or the purchase of photographic prints,
contact Paul Gilbert at:

Wild Light Press
135-4800 No. 3 Rd., Suite 125, Richmond, B.C. V6X 3A6